65 Flavorful, Stress-Free Recipes

GOURMET Indoor GRILLING

MATT PELTON

FRONT TABLE BOOKS

AN IMPRINT OF CEDAR FORT, INC. | SPRINGVILLE, UTAH

I dedicate this book to Aviana, without whom many of the recipes, inspiration, and imaginations would not have been nearly as brilliant. Thank you for all that you do. You are the most creative and imaginative chef I have ever known, and together with my technical skills, we can create the most amazing things. You are my greatest inspiration.

—Matthew

ISBN 13: 978-1-4621-2270-7

Published by Front Table Books, an imprint of Cedar Fort, Inc.
2373 W. 700 S., Springville, UT 84663
Distributed by Cedar Fort, Inc., www.cedarfort.com

Library of Congress Control Number: 2018952395

Cover design by Shawnda T. Craig
Page design by Shawnda T. Craig
Cover design © 2018 Cedar Fort, Inc.
Edited by Kaitlin Barwick

Printed in the United States of America

10 9 8 7 6 5 4 3 2 1

Printed on acid-free paper

CONTENTS

GOURMET SANDWICHES 111

GRILLED DESSERTS 121

CONCLUSION 132

INDEX 133

ABOUT THE AUTHOR 138

INTRODUCTION

GRILLING FOOD is an exciting way to create amazing food. The carbonized edges from the grill along with the beautiful caramelization create depth and bring flavors to our food that we don't otherwise experience. Oftentimes, we think of grilling as only a warm-weather activity and, in particular, a summertime event. This book was created to break that trend and open up the idea that grilling can be done anytime. There are now many indoor grilling options, from electric countertop models to cast-iron grills built into gas ranges.

INSPIRATION FROM CULTURES

In this book, we have put together grilling recipes inspired from all over the world. All cultures have some connections to grilling because of the primal nature of cooking food over fire. We have studied these cultures and their connections to food. We have found that grilling is the one universal cooking technique that is present in every culture. A number of the recipes in this book are inspired by these cultures and give homage to the foods while incorporating techniques and ingredients that are familiar to our own culture.

WHOLE FRESH FOOD

Our recipes and books revolve around using fresh whole ingredients and techniques. Our culture today has become so disconnected from our food that we barely understand what is good for us and what is damaging. We have a constant onslaught of faster and more convenient foods, and what we end up fueling our bodies with is causing massive health problems. The goal of this book is to help connect people to their food, show them how to use fresh and whole ingredients, and let them experience the feelings for themselves. We always recommend buying local source, organic, GMO-free ingredients and supporting local small producers. Not only will your health be benefited, the food will taste better, and the local economy will be supported. There has been a large shift in our culture to move toward this, and we want to always promote and be at the forefront of it as well.

WHY INDOOR GRILLING

Grilling indoors allows you to enjoy this cooking method at all times of the year, not just summer. It is not a method that has been explored much. There has been a push toward it, and we hope this book helps move it further. Indoor grilling is also a great option for those living in small apartments or urban areas where a traditional back-patio grill is not permitted or there is no room for it. With the many indoor models available, this can be a great option. Grilling food enhances flavors and brings out new and exciting flavors not available in other cooking methods. In addition to great flavors, grilling is a healthier way to cook without all the fats needed in other methods.

INDOOR GRILLS

There are several varieties of indoor grills, some of the more popular include cast iron, Korean BBQ, hibachi, and George Foreman (electric grill).

CAST IRON

Cast-iron grills are either a built-in grill on a number of new gas ranges or a portable grill pan that can be used on any stovetop. The advantage of cast iron is that you can get it very hot and set deep grill marks into whatever you want to grill. Cast-iron grills also offer a healthy advantage of iron from the grill that enters you food as it cooks, giving you access to that important mineral that is often difficult to get enough of.

KOREAN BBQ

The Korean BBQ grills are generally a grill plate set on top of a butane tabletop burner. These can be picked up at most Asian markets for a very reasonable price. They can be used for grilling anything you want—not just Asian food. In my opinion, they are the very best option for the price and should definitely not be looked over.

HIBACHI

Hibachi grills are traditionally wood coal burning, which is not always feasible in a living space. Today, there are electric hibachi options that work really well indoors. Like the Korean, there is no need to be pigeonholed in cooking only Asian foods; this grill will work well with any type of grilling.

GEORGE FOREMAN

Electric countertop grills like the George Foreman are quite popular and make grilling indoors a breeze. Billed as a healthier way to cook, these grills are easy to use and provide easy storage and portability.

PROTEIN LIKE A PRO

In this chapter, I will go into step-by-step detail on each of the proteins using only salt and pepper to season, letting the protein speak for itself. From these basics, you can create a number of amazing dishes that will enhance any dinner party.

There are several key factors that are very important when picking out meat at a store. If you start with great fresh ingredients, the end result will be so much better. The following is a list of what to look for when picking out some of the major proteins at the market.

Beef: Beef is the most common grilled meat in America. It may be our diet tendencies or the ease of grilling, but there is something about the smell of a burger or a steak on the grill that people can relate to. When looking for beef, there are several things to look for:

First, the tenderness and age of the beef. If you look at a steak of any sort, it should look like it has decent color to it. If it appears to be brown in the package, avoid it.

Marbling: This is typically only something to look for in higher-end cuts, such as a ribeye or a New York steak, but it is important for other beef cuts as well. Marbling is the interior muscle fat. It looks like white specks or striations in the meat. People generally think that the more fat the better, but that is not always the case. The higher-quality beef will have more of the white specks, but they will be smaller and more evenly spread out. Also feel the marbling in the meat, if it feels hard and plasticky, it will not render well and will just remain fatty. If it is waxy and can be pressed in with your finger, it is a better quality and will render well, making the meat more flavorful.

The next thing you want to look for is the age of the beef. As beef ages, enzymes slowly break down the meat and allow it to become tender. If you press down into the center of a piece of beef, it should dimple, and the dimple should stay in the meat for several seconds.

If the color is good, the marbling looks good, and it dimples, it is a good-quality cut of beef. For ground beef, look for good coloring and the proper fat to meat ratio. I prefer an 80/20 mix as it will add flavor but not leave the burger greasy. Any less fat and the burger seems to fall apart. More fat and you get a greasy burger.

Pork: With pork, color is key. The pork should be vibrant and fresh, ranging from light pink in color to bright red. The juices should always be clear. If the juices are cloudy at all, the pork has turned and should be avoided at all costs. The pork should dimple but only for a couple of seconds. Pork generally does not have the marbling of beef, and if it does, it should be very fine.

Chicken: Chicken should be bright and fresh looking like pork, with a good shine to the meat. Like pork, the juices should be absolutely clear, and when pressed, the chicken should spring back immediately. If it dimples at all, pass it by.

Fish: Fish is the most delicate of all the protein groups. Fish should be bright, fresh, and shiny and should absolutely bounce back quickly when pressed with your finger. If you are looking at whole fish, observe the skin and the eyes—both should appear to be bright. All other seafood should follow similar guidelines.

With cooking proteins, I recommend using a quick digital thermometer probe. These are relatively inexpensive on Amazon and will make a huge difference in your cooking by taking the guesswork out. I recommend Thermoworks thermometers out of any available; they are always fast and accurate and don't need to be recalibrated.

Cook proteins to the following USDA-recommended internal temperatures. Make sure to check in the very center portion and give it a few seconds to record. If it is a critical temperature for safety, like poultry items, probe it in several spots in the thickest areas and near the bones to make sure that you are safe.

- Beef (not ground): 135 degrees (medium rare)
- Beef (ground): 155 degrees (medium well)
- Pork (not ground): 145 degrees
- Pork (ground): 155 degrees
- Poultry (dark meat): 175 degrees
- Poultry (white meat): 165 degrees
- Fish: 125 degrees
- Wild meat: 145 degrees
- Stuffed meats: 155 degrees

PROTEIN LIKE A PRO

PROTEINS ARE THE MOST COMMON grilled food items and what most people think about when they think about grilling. In this chapter, I will teach you techniques that will have you grilling proteins like a pro and enhancing all of your grilling experience. Most of the following recipes use only salt and pepper, and there are no amounts. This is to show that the proteins are able to speak for themselves and that it's more the technique than the recipe that makes the difference.

STEAK RIBEYE/NEW YORK

Ribeye and New York steaks are the most common steaks for grilling due to their high fat content and the fact that they often turn out well regardless of how well they are cooked. A little technique can go a long way in creating an amazing meat following these instructions.

ribeye or New York steaks, about 1 inch thick

salt and pepper to taste

1. Salt the outside of the steak evenly on both sides, then do the same with the pepper.
2. Let the steak relax at room temperature for 10 minutes.
3. Heat up your indoor grill to high, and spray it with spray oil.
4. Place the steaks on the hot grill, and cook them for 3 minutes per side. The steak should pull from the grill easily. If it doesn't, leave it on the grill for more time until it does.
5. Remove the steaks and set them to the side to relax at room temperature for several minutes. This will allow the juice to redistribute and allow for even cooking. Turn the grill down to medium.
6. Return the steaks to the grill, rotating the grill marks, and grill them for several minutes per side. The internal temperature should be 130 degrees for medium rare, 140 for medium, 145 for medium well, and 155 for well done.
7. Remove the steaks from the grill and let them relax for 5–7 minutes before slicing to serve.

HAMBURGER

Burgers and grills have gone together from the start. There is something magical about a family gathering in the summertime with grilled burgers. Once you learn the art of a great burger, you can start to experiment with stuffed burgers and other fun ideas.

80/20 ground beef

salt and pepper to taste

1. Form the ground beef into burger patties about 1 inch thick, slightly domed in the center and slightly larger than the diameter of the buns you are going to serve them on.
2. Season with salt and pepper, and let the patties relax at room temperature for several minutes.
3. Heat up your indoor grill to high.
4. Place the burgers on the grill, and cook them for 3–4 minutes per side. The burgers should remove easily from the grill racks.
5. Turn the grill down to medium and finish the burger to an internal temperature of 150 degrees.
6. Let the burgers relax for 5 minutes before serving.

LONDON BROIL

A London broil is a thick-cut top round steak that is marinated for several hours before being grilled and sliced thin. It has been largely overshadowed as of late by the tri-tip, which is prepared in the same manner.

1 (2.5-lb.) London broil or tri-tip

1 cup soy sauce

3 cloves garlic, peeled and kept whole

1 onion, sliced large

2 tsp. black pepper

¼ cup packed brown sugar

1. Prepare the marinade by combining the soy sauce, garlic, onion, pepper, and brown sugar in a glass bowl or large resealable bag. Place the London broil in the marinade and refrigerate for several hours or overnight.

2. Heat up your indoor grill to high, and spray it with spray oil.

3. Place the London broil on the hot grill, and cook for 10 minutes per side. The meat should pull away from the grill easily. If it doesn't, leave it on the grill for more time until it does.

4. Remove the London broil and set it to the side to relax at room temperature for several minutes. This will allow the juice to redistribute and allow for even cooking. Turn the grill down to medium.

5. Return the London broil to the grill, rotating the grill marks, and grill it for about 30 minutes. The internal temperature should be 130 degrees for medium rare, 140 for medium, 145 for medium well, and 155 for well done.

6. Remove the London broil from the grill, and let it relax for 5–7 minutes before slicing to serve.

CHICKEN BREAST

Chicken breast is one of the hardest proteins to do well on a grill. It dries out easily and quickly, and the lack of fats make it very unforgiving. Follow these steps, however, and you will be cooking chicken breasts like a pro on the grill.

boneless, skinless chicken breasts, leveled out
   to a similar thickness

olive oil

salt and pepper to taste

1. Brush the chicken breasts with the olive oil until they are coated liberally.
2. Add salt and pepper to taste, and let the breasts relax at room temperature for about 10 minutes.
3. Heat the grill up to high, and spray it with spray oil.
4. Cook the chicken breasts for about 3 minutes per side. The breasts should not stick to the grill. If they do, continue to cook until they pull away clean.
5. Remove the breasts from the grill and let them relax for several minutes to allow the juices to redistribute.
6. Turn the grill to medium heat.
7. Return the breasts to the grill, and cook them until the internal temperature is 160 degrees (they will continue to cook after you remove them from the heat until they are over 165 degrees).
8. Let the breasts relax for 5–10 minutes before cutting and serving.

BONE-IN CHICKEN

Bone-in chicken on the grill is generally legs and thighs but can also refer to breasts and wings. There is a very different process to cooking bone-in rather than the chicken breasts as described in the previous recipe. In this recipe, I am describing using chicken thighs. The only difference to grill different cuts of bone-in meat will be the time it takes to cook.

bone-in, skin-on chicken thighs

olive oil

salt and pepper to taste

BBQ sauce

1. Brush the chicken thighs with the olive oil liberally and season with salt and pepper. Let them relax at room temperature for 10 minutes.
2. Heat the grill up to high.
3. Place the thighs skin-side down, and cook for 5 minutes or until the thighs pull away cleanly from the grill.
4. Turn the thighs bone-side down, and turn the grill down to medium heat.
5. Cook for about 20 minutes or until the temperature near the bone is 170 degrees.
6. Brush the thighs with BBQ sauce, and let them stay on the grill for 2–3 minutes to set the sauce.
7. Let the thighs relax for several minutes before serving.

PORK CHOPS

Unfortunately, throughout my life I have been served a lot of grilled pork chops so overdone on the grill you could shingle a roof with them. A lot of people have it in their mind that pork needs to be cooked to burned to be safe to eat. The USDA recommends that pork be cooked to 145 degrees to be safe (this is the point of a steak cooked to medium well). At 145 degrees, the center of the pork chop will be very slightly pink. At 150 degrees, the meat will be white all the way through but still moist. I do not ever recommend cooking pork beyond this point.

pork chops, cut 1 inch thick

salt and pepper to taste

1. Salt and pepper the outside of the pork chops evenly on both sides.
2. Let the pork chops relax at room temperature for 10 minutes.
3. Heat up your indoor grill to high, and spray it with spray oil.
4. Place the pork chops on the hot grill and cook them for 3 minutes per side or until the meat pulls away from the grill easily.
5. Remove the pork chops and set them to the side to relax at room temperature for several minutes. This will allow the juice to redistribute and allow for even cooking. Turn the grill down to medium.
6. Return the pork chops to the grill, rotating the grill marks, and grill them for several minutes per side. The internal temperature should be 145 degrees.
7. Remove the pork chops from the grill, and let them relax for 5–7 minutes before slicing to serve.

PORK LOIN ROAST

This recipe refers to the pork top loin, where the pork chops are generally cut. I have described cooking this with just salt, pepper, and marmalade, but you can experiment with whatever you would like.

1 (3-lb.) pork top loin roast

Kosher salt

black pepper to taste

orange marmalade

1. Remove any silver skin and excess fat from the loin. Trim the loin to be even in thickness throughout.
2. Coat the loin with Kosher salt liberally, place in a resealable bag, and refrigerate for at least 3 hours or overnight. This will dry brine the roast and keep it moist while it cooks.
3. Rinse the excess salt off the roast, pat it dry, and season it with black pepper.
4. Turn the grill on to high, and spray it with spray oil.
5. Cook the loin on high for several minutes per side until it pulls cleanly from the grill.
6. Remove the loin from the grill and allow it to relax for several minutes to allow the juices to redistribute.
7. Turn the grill down to medium, and return the loin to the grill. Cook for about 30 minutes, turning occasionally, until the internal temperature reaches 145 degrees.
8. Glaze the outside of the loin with the marmalade, and let it relax for at least 10 minutes before slicing and serving.

PORK BABY BACK RIBS

Years ago on a river bank in Alaska, I tasted the best-tasting ribs I have ever had. I was fascinated and learned a process to cook ribs that turn out tender, moist, and delicious. Everyone tries to cook them with the meat side toward the heat, but the best way is to cook them with the bone side to the heat, as that is the natural way heat is distributed through the ribs.

2 lbs. baby back ribs

olive oil

salt and pepper to taste

BBQ sauce

1. Remove the membrane from the bone side of the ribs. Coat with olive oil and sprinkle with salt and pepper. Let stand for 10 minutes.
2. Heat up the grill to medium, and place the ribs bone side to the heat. Cook for 1.5 hours or until the temperature is 190–195 degrees.
3. Remove the ribs from the grill and let them relax for 30 minutes.
4. Brush the ribs with BBQ sauce, and place on a hot grill for 2–3 minutes to set the sauce before serving.

PORK TENDERLOIN

In my opinion, pork tenderloin is one of the most underrated proteins. It is one of my favorite proteins to cook, and it definitely deserves more recognition.

pork tenderloin

olive oil

salt and pepper to taste

1. Remove the silver skin and fat from the pork tenderloin and trim to a similar thickness.
2. Brush with olive oil and sprinkle with salt and pepper.
3. Heat up the grill to high, and cook for 3–4 minutes per side or until the meat removes easily from the grill.
4. Remove the tenderloins from the grill and let them relax for several minutes.
5. Turn the grill to medium and return the tenderloins to the grill. Cook for 15–20 minutes or until the temperature is 145 degrees.
6. Remove the tenderloins from the grill, and let them relax for several minutes before serving.

AHI TUNA

The first time I had ahi tuna, I was a little skeptical eating what seemed like sushi. It was grilled with a sesame soy crust and seared hard and just warmed in the middle. I learned that the fats are delicate and delicious, and they are lost when cooked through.

ahi steaks, cut about 1.5 inches thick

soy sauce

brown sugar

toasted sesame seeds

1. Preheat the indoor grill to the highest setting.
2. Drizzle the soy sauce followed by the brown sugar on both sides of the ahi steaks.
3. Roll the steaks in the sesame seeds.
4. Spray the grill with spray oil.
5. Grill the ahi steaks for 2–3 minutes per side.
6. Let the steaks relax for 5 minutes.
7. Slice thin and serve. Drizzle with more soy sauce if desired.

SWORDFISH

Swordfish, when cooked correctly, is one of my favorite proteins. It has a firm, moist texture and is mild in flavor.

swordfish fillets, cut about 1.5 inches thick

olive oil

sea salt and pepper to taste

1. Preheat the grill to high.
2. Drizzle the fillets with olive oil and season with sea salt and black pepper.
3. Place on the grill and cook for 3 minutes per side.
4. Turn the grill down to medium and continue grilling for 5 minutes per side or until the sides of the swordfish are homogeneous in color.
5. Let the fish relax for 5 minutes before serving.

HALIBUT

Overall, halibut is the most versatile fish you can cook. Whether fried, sautéed, or grilled, it's an amazing protein that is mild, flaky, and moist. The only struggle is the lack of fats, so the fish can dry out if you aren't careful. You can combat this by cooking it extremely hot brushed with oil.

halibut fillets, cut about 1 inch thick

olive oil

sea salt and pepper

fresh grated parmesan cheese

fresh chopped parsley

fresh lemon juice

1. Brush the halibut fillets with the olive oil and sprinkle with the salt and pepper.
2. Preheat the grill to high.
3. Spray the grill with spray oil, and immediately place the halibut on the heat.
4. Grill for 2 minutes per side.
5. Turn the grill down to medium, and grill for 2 minutes per side.
6. Sprinkle the halibut with the parmesan, and grill an additional minute before removing from the heat.
7. Sprinkle the fillets with parsley and lemon juice, and let it relax for 5 minutes before serving.

SALMON

Salmon is my all-time favorite protein. There are many types of salmon, and the debate goes on forever on which is the best. My personal favorite is Coho salmon, but the freshness and the preparation of the salmon is more important than the type.

boneless salmon fillets, scaled

olive oil

sea salt and pepper to taste

1. Preheat the grill to high.
2. Drizzle the fillets with olive oil and season with sea salt and black pepper.
3. Place on the grill, and cook for 3 minutes per side.
4. Turn the grill down to medium and continue grilling for several minutes until the fillet is homogeneous in color and white is beginning to appear on top of the fillet.
5. Remove from heat, and let it rest for a few minutes before serving.

SCALLOPS

Scallops are so amazing and delicate. My first introduction to this protein was when I cooked the fresh scallops I caught in tide pools in Alaska. I expected something akin to clams in texture, but I was pleasantly surprised by how chewy and soft scallops were. They have become my favorite shellfish.

large fresh bay scallops

real butter, melted

sea salt and pepper to taste

1. Preheat the grill to high.
2. Melt the butter, and set it aside so that it is ready for later.
3. Season the scallops with salt and pepper.
4. Spray the grill with spray oil, and immediately place the scallops on the heat. Brush the tops with butter.
5. Grill for 3–4 minutes per side, brushing with the butter again after flipping. The scallops are ready to turn when they pull away easily from the grill.
6. Brush the scallops again with the butter, and grill for an additional thirty seconds per side.
7. Let the scallops relax for 5 minutes before serving.

SHRIMP

Shrimp is probably the most common grilled seafood. They are easy to grill and even easier to tell when they are done. Raw shrimp will appear gray and blue. Cooked shrimp will be white and pink.

large raw shrimp, peeled and mud vein removed

olive oil

garlic salt to taste

fresh lime juice

1. Preheat the grill to high.
2. Place the shrimp on the skewers through the center in the same direction.
3. Brush with olive oil and sprinkle with garlic salt.
4. Place the skewers on the grill and cook for 2 minutes on each side or until the half toward the heat has turned pink and white.
5. Drizzle with the lime juice, and grill a few seconds per side.
6. Remove from heat and serve immediately.

GOURMET VEGETARIAN GRILLING

I OFTEN FEEL THAT MEAT is the only star of the grill. This is certainly the case in many United States homes, but I believe that vegetables are making a resurgence as a go-to for grilling. Grilling brings such a beautiful caramelized layer to the vegetables that I can't believe that it is not done more often.

GRILLED YELLOW POTATOES 39

GRILLED STUFFED PORTABELLA CAPS 40

GRILLED SUMMER SQUASH 43

ELOTE (SPANISH CORN ON THE COB) 44

GRILLED EGGPLANT NAPOLEON 45

GRILLED SWEET POTATOES 46

GRILLED ARTICHOKES WITH HONEY DIJON 49

GRILLED BRUSSELS SPROUTS WITH BALSAMIC GLAZE 50

GRILLED BBQ TOFU 51

GRILLED YELLOW POTATOES

Not many people have ever grilled potatoes, but once you have tried them, grilling will become your favorite way of cooking them. I like to serve the grilled potatoes with a protein choice like salmon, chicken, beef, or pork for a delicious balanced meal. Make sure to always use "waxy" small potatoes. These potatoes have a high sugar content and will hold together while being grilled—the starchy large potatoes will just fall apart. Waxy potatoes are often white, yellow, or red, but never brown. If they are larger than your palm, they will be too starchy for grilling.

yellow potatoes

olive oil

sea salt and black pepper to taste

paprika

1. Slice the potatoes in half lengthwise, and place them into a large bag or bowl.
2. Drizzle them with olive oil, and stir or shake to coat the potatoes.
3. Add the salt, pepper, and paprika to taste, and stir or shake until completely combined.
4. Preheat the grill to medium, and spray it with oil.
5. Place the potatoes sliced-side down, and grill for several minutes or until you can see grill marks and they feel tender on the cut side.
6. Turn the potatoes over and grill until they are tender through.
7. Remove from heat and serve.

GRILLED STUFFED PORTABELLA CAPS

I was introduced to grilled portabella caps twenty years ago. They were so amazing, I could barely contain myself and ate way too many.

portabella mushroom caps

olive oil

sea salt to taste

kale

garlic cloves

sweet onion

cherry tomatoes

shredded parmesan cheese

balsamic vinegar

1. Remove the stems from the mushrooms. Brush the remaining caps with olive oil and sprinkle with sea salt.
2. Finely mince the kale, garlic, and onion. Sauté them in olive oil until the kale is becoming tender.
3. Line the portabella caps with the tomatoes around the inner edge, and fill the center with the kale mixture. Sprinkle the top with the parmesan. Heat the grill to medium, and grill the caps for 10 minutes or until the cheese is starting to melt.
4. Drizzle the caps with balsamic vinegar and serve on the rind brushed with butter.

GRILLED SUMMER SQUASH

I love summer squash, like yellow squash and zucchini. Grilling them is one of my favorite tastes of summer.

summer squash
olive oil
sea salt to taste

1. Slice the squash in half lengthwise. Brush the squash with the olive oil and season with salt.
2. Heat the grill to medium heat, and set the squash cut-side down. Cook for 5 minutes per side until it is tender.
3. Remove from heat and serve.

ELOTE (SPANISH CORN ON THE COB)

I was a bit skeptical the first time I tried an elote. I love grilled corn on the cob, but I just wasn't sure about the mayo and chili lime powder. The effect was amazing though—it may be my favorite way to eat corn.

corn on the cob
olive oil
sea salt to taste
mayonnaise
Tepín chili lime salt*
grated parmesan cheese

1. Remove the corn from the husk.
2. Brush with olive oil and sprinkle with sea salt.
3. Heat the grill to high, and grill for several minutes, turning the corn over as needed. The corn is done when it begins to wrinkle.
4. Brush with mayo and sprinkle with chili lime salt and parmesan cheese to serve.

* Tepín is sold at most Latin markets. You can also substitute with creole seasoning.

GRILLED EGGPLANT NAPOLEON

I think eggplant is often overlooked as a great vegetable. I love eggplant, especially grilled. Haloumi is a firm greek cheese that is often grilled and is available in specialty cheese markets.

1 Eggplant sliced lengthwise into half inch slices
Olive Oil brushed
Salt to taste
Heirloom Tomatoes sliced thin
Lemon squeezed
Balsamic Vinegar drizzled
Fresh Basil garnished
Haloumi cheese sliced to ¼ inch thick and grilled

1. Slice the eggplant thin lengthwise and brush with the olive oil and season with the sea salt.
2. Slice the Halloumi to ¼ inch and grill on high for one minute per side
3. Turn the grill on high and grill the eggplant for several minutes per side until the grill marks are prevalent.
4. Layer with the eggplant with grilled halloumi, and sliced tomatoes. Squeeze the lemon juice over the top, drizzle the balsamic vinegar, and garnish with slightly torn fresh basil.

GRILLED SWEET POTATOES

Very similar in cooking to the grilled yellow potatoes, this is a different way to prepare sweet potatoes that brings a whole new dimension to the ingredient.

sweet potatoes
olive oil
sea salt to taste

1. Slice the sweet potatoes in half lengthwise.
2. Brush the entire sweet potato with olive oil and season liberally with sea salt.
3. Heat the grill to high, and grill the sweet potatoes cut-side down for 5–7 minutes. Turn them over and grill on medium heat until the sweet potatoes are tender through.
4. Let the potatoes relax for several minutes before serving.

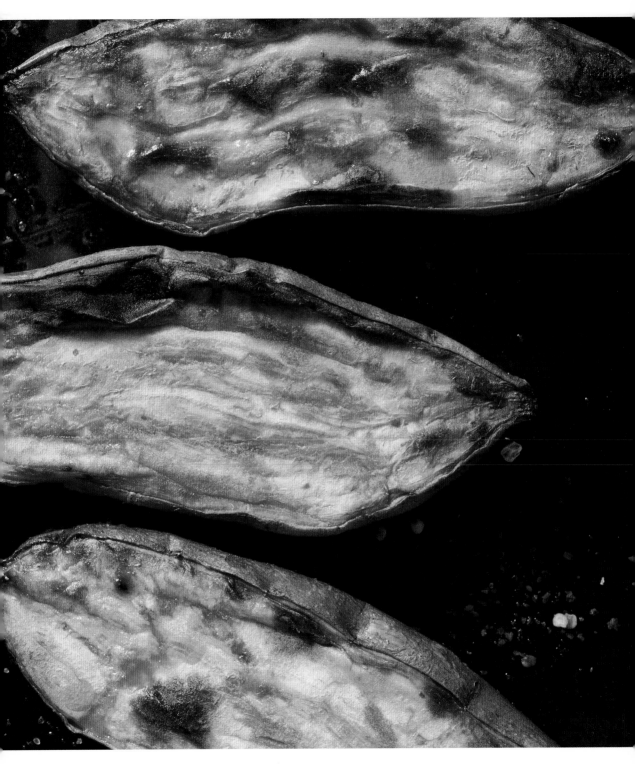

GRILLED ARTICHOKES WITH HONEY DIJON

Artichokes are amazing, and I think it's sad that most people have only had them steamed or boiled. The grill is the best way to cook these for ultimate flavor.

6 whole artichokes
½ gallon water
3 Tbsp. sea salt
olive oil
sea salt to taste
¼ cup raw honey
¼ cup boiling water
3 Tbsp. Dijon mustard

1. Cut the artichokes in half lengthwise top to bottom.
2. Mix the 3 tablespoons of sea salt and water together. Place the artichokes in the brine for 30 minutes to several hours before cooking.
3. Heat the grill to medium.
4. Remove the artichokes from the brine, drizzle with olive oil on the cut side, and season with sea salt.
5. Grill for 15 minutes on each side, cut side down first.
6. Turn the grill down to low, and turn the artichokes cut-side down while you mix the honey, boiling water, and Dijon.
7. Turn the artichokes back over, and brush the Dijon mix well over the cut side until it is all absorbed.
8. Serve alongside a protein like salmon, beef, pork, or chicken, or with rice or potatoes for a vegetarian option.

GRILLED BRUSSELS SPROUTS WITH BALSAMIC GLAZE

I love grilled brussels sprouts. I think there is a depth of flavor that you only get from the grill.

brussels sprouts
olive oil
sea salt to taste
balsamic vinegar

1. Cut the sprouts in half lengthwise from top to bottom.
2. Brush with olive oil and season with sea salt.
3. Heat the grill to high, and grill the sprouts cut-side down for 5 minutes on each side.
4. Brush the sprouts lightly with balsamic, and grill for a minute or so more to set the vinegar before serving.

GRILLED BBQ TOFU

Because of tofu's texture and lack of flavor, I was never a big fan of it. But while learning to cook Asian cuisine, I had to learn to embrace it. There are definitely ways to manipulate the texture, and the flavor can be whatever you want it to be.

firm tofu

olive oil

sea salt to taste

BBQ sauce

1. Cut the tofu into 1-inch strips, and freeze them.
2. Place the frozen tofu strips on a cookie sheet that is covered with paper towels. Layer more paper towels on top of the tofu, and place another cookie sheet on top. Add weight to press the liquid out of the tofu as it thaws.
3. Once the tofu is completely thawed, brush the strips with olive oil and sea salt.
4. Heat the grill to high, and grill the strips for 10 minutes per side.
5. Brush with BBQ sauce, and return them to the grill for a couple of minutes to set the sauce before serving.

UNIQUE WORLD GRILLING

THE FOLLOWING CHAPTERS are grilling techniques and recipes from around the world. Grilling is the most primal way to cook, and every culture in the world has a different flavor profile or unique taste. We have had a lot of fun putting this section of the book together. The recipes are fantastic as we interpreted the world flavors into dishes for the indoor grill.

CHURRASCO

MY FIRST EXPERIENCE WITH A CHURRASCO meal was in the mid '90s. I was a teenager, and there was a restaurant that served all-you-can-eat grilled meat. I was hooked immediately.

BACON-WRAPPED CHICKEN 54

FLANK STEAK WITH CHIMICHURRI 57

CARNE ASADA 58

GRILLED PINEAPPLE WITH CINNAMON HONEY 61

PARMESAN GARLIC BEEF 62

CACAO-RUBBED HANGAR STEAK 63

BACON-WRAPPED CHICKEN

This is a simple and very tasty churrasco dish. The bacon pairs well with the chicken and keeps it moist while adding a layer of crispness.

boneless, skinless chicken breasts
uncooked bacon
salt and pepper to taste

1. Cut the chicken breasts into bite-sized chunks, and lightly season with salt and pepper.
2. Wrap the bacon strips once around the chicken chunks, and place them on a skewer.
3. Heat the grill to high, and grill the skewers for several minutes per side. The bacon should be crispy and the chicken white.
4. Let the skewers relax for 5 minutes before serving.

FLANK STEAK WITH CHIMICHURRI

This is one of my favorite ways to eat grilled steaks. The chimichurri sauce is very lovely with the grilled beef. This chimichurri sauce recipe will cover up to 5 lbs. of steak.

Ingredients for the steak
flank steak

olive oil

sea salt

black pepper

smoked sweet paprika

For the chimichurri
1 bunch fresh parsley

4 cloves garlic

2 sprigs fresh oregano

2 Tbsp. red wine vinegar

3 Tbsp. olive oil

2 tsp. of sea salt

1. Mix the ingredients for the chimichurri in a food processor until smooth.
2. Season the flank steak strips with the olive oil, salt, pepper, and paprika.
3. Heat the grill to high, and cook the strips for 2 minutes per side.
4. Let the meat relax for a few minutes. Coat with the chimichurri sauce and serve.

CARNE ASADA

Like the chimichurri, the flank steak is the choice for this recipe, though any large, thin-cut beef will work. Carne asada is mainly served in tortillas as tacos.

2 lbs. flank steak

1 cup orange juice

2 limes, squeezed and zested

1 onion, sliced into rings

1 tsp. cumin

2 tsp. New Mexico chili powder

3 tsp. sea salt

1. Mix all the ingredients together in a resealable bag, and refrigerate for 3 hours to overnight.
2. Heat the grill to high, and grill the steak for several minutes per side.
3. Relax for 5 minutes before slicing thin. Eat with tortillas as a taco dressed as you like.

GRILLED PINEAPPLE WITH CINNAMON HONEY

When I was first introduced to grilled pineapple, I couldn't believe how good it was! Now I crave grilled pineapple all the time. The natural sugars of the fruit are enhanced through the grilling process.

fresh pineapple

raw honey

cinnamon

1. Slice the pineapple into 1-inch spears. Place them on skewers if desired.
2. Drizzle the pineapple spears with honey and cinnamon on both sides.
3. Heat the grill to high, and grill for several minutes on each side.

PARMESAN GARLIC BEEF

There is nothing too fancy about this recipe, but the results are amazing.

2 lbs. sirloin beef, cut into 1-inch cubes
6 garlic cloves, finely minced
¼ cup olive oil
sea salt to taste
¼ cup grated parmesan

1. Mix the ingredients together and place them in a covered bowl or bag in the fridge for 3 hours to overnight.
2. Place the beef chunks onto skewers.
3. Heat the grill to high, and grill for about 3 minutes per side, sprinkling each side with parmesan. Grill for a few minutes more until it's done to the point you like it.
4. Let the meat relax for several minutes before serving.

CACAO-RUBBED HANGAR STEAK

I had this the first time at a brilliant restaurant in Michigan. It is quite tasty and is perfectly suited for the grill.

2 lbs. hangar steak
¼ cup olive oil
sea salt to taste
cacao nibs

1. Brush the hangar steak with the olive oil and coat with the sea salt and cacao nibs.
2. Heat the grill to high, and grill for 2 minutes per side.
3. Remove it from the grill, and let the meat relax for several minutes before serving.

KOREAN BBQ

IT WOULD BE A SHAME to have an indoor grilling book and not include Korean BBQ. Korean BBQ can trace its roots to Goguryeo, one of the earliest Korean Kingdoms in the first century A.D. and the dish neobiani which later became bulgogi. Indoor grilling is a cultural coming together, everyone enjoying the fire and cooking together.

BEEF BULGOGI 66

KOREAN SPICY PORK 68

KALBI SHORT RIBS 69

CHICKEN BULGOGI 70

KOREAN PANCAKES 71

BEEF BULGOGI

This is one of my very favorite ways to grill beef. The sweet and spicy thin-cut steaks are quite tasty served with rice and kimchi.

2 lbs. flank steak

½ cup soy sauce

½ cup brown sugar

2 Tbsp. chopped green onion

4 cloves garlic, minced

2 Tbsp. sesame seeds

2 Tbsp. sesame oil

2 tsp. black pepper

1. Mix all of the ingredients together in a bowl or bag and refrigerate for several hours to overnight.
2. Heat the grill to high, and grill the steak for several minutes per side until it is at your preferred doneness.
3. Let rest for several minutes before slicing and serving.

KOREAN SPICY PORK

Like beef bulgogi, the pork bulgogi (often called spicy pork) is very much a staple of Korean BBQ.

2 lbs. pork, cut into ⅛-inch slices

½ cup soy sauce

5 cloves garlic, minced

3 Tbsp. minced green onion

1 yellow onion, sliced

2 Tbsp. sesame seeds

3 tsp. black pepper

½ cup brown sugar

3 Tbsp. gochujang (Korean red chili paste)

red pepper flakes to taste

1. Mix all the ingredients together in a covered glass bowl or resealable bag and refrigerate for several hours to overnight.
2. Heat the grill to high, and grill the pork for 2–3 minutes per side until it is cooked through.
3. Serve immediately on rice or lettuce leaves with soy and/or kimchi.

KALBI SHORT RIBS

Kalbi short ribs are a favorite all around the Polynesian islands as well as in Korea.

3 lbs. beef short ribs

½ cup brown sugar

½ cup soy sauce

¼ cup mirin

1 small onion, sliced

1 Asian pear, diced small

4 cloves garlic, minced

3 Tbsp. sesame oil

2 tsp. black pepper

2 Tbsp. minced green onions

1. Mix all the ingredients together in a covered glass bowl or resealable bag and refrigerate for several hours to overnight.
2. Heat the grill to high and grill the ribs for 3–5 minutes per side until they are cooked through.

CHICKEN BULGOGI

Like the beef bulgogi, this is a staple in Korean BBQ. The sweet chicken is delicious.

3 lbs. boneless, skinless chicken thighs

½ cup soy sauce

2 Tbsp. Korean chili paste or sriracha

¼ cup brown sugar

¼ cup mirin

4 cloves garlic, minced

3 Tbsp. sesame oil

2 tsp. fresh grated ginger

2 tsp. black pepper

1 Tbsp. sesame seeds

1. Mix all the ingredients together in a covered glass bowl or resealable bag and refrigerate for several hours to overnight.
2. Heat the grill to high and grill the chicken thighs for several minutes per side until it is cooked through.
3. Let rest for several minutes before slicing thin and serving.

KOREAN PANCAKES

These are my favorite Korean treat, full of veggies and kimchi.
They are amazing grilled and served with the Korean BBQ.

2 eggs

½ cup cold water

2 tsp. salt

1 tsp. baking powder

1 cup flour

¼ cup tapioca flour

¼ cup bean sprouts

¼ cup kimchi

3 Tbsp. chopped green onion

1. Mix the eggs and water together. Stir in the salt, baking powder, and flour slowly. It should make a thick, pasty batter.
2. Fold in the tapioca flour, bean sprouts, kimchi, and green onion.
3. Heat the grill to medium.
4. Place parchment paper on the grill and spray the paper with spray oil.
5. Spoon the batter onto the parchment paper and cook the pancakes until you see the edges start to brown. Flip them and cook through.
6. Serve with Korean BBQ protein selections and grilled vegetables like mushrooms and summer squash and drizzled with soy sauce.

ASIAN

A HIBACHI GRILL is a teaditional Japanese grill often made from cast iron. It uses wood coals for fuel and sits on top pf a table in a well ventilated area. Recently, tgere have been several electric models built and most of your indoor grills are well suited to grill Hibachi dishes

CITRUS AND GINGER SPATCHCOCK CHICKEN 74

HIBACHI CHICKEN 77

HIBACHI SALMON 78

HIBACHI STEAK 79

HIBACHI SHRIMP 80

ASIAN ZOODLES 83

CITRUS AND GINGER SPATCHCOCK CHICKEN

You can substitute game hen, pheasant, or quail for this recipe. This is so good and moist. When you spatchcock the chicken, it cooks very evenly.

1 small roasting hen (or 2 game hens)

1 cup orange juice

½ cup soy sauce

¼ cup mirin

1 Tbsp. fresh grated ginger

1 tsp. black pepper

3 cloves garlic, finely minced

1. To spatchcock, cut the backbone out of the bird and press the bird flat.
2. Mix the remaining ingredients together and combine with the hen in a covered glass bowl or resealable bag. Refrigerate for several hours to overnight.
3. Heat the grill to high, and grill the hen bone-side down for 20 minutes or until the meat in the thighs reaches 170 degrees.
4. Let rest for 10 minutes before serving whole.

HIBACHI CHICKEN

When grilled on the hibachi, the teriyaki flavor of this chicken is enhanced. It is my favorite way to eat it.

2 lbs. chicken breast sliced thin

½ cup teriyaki sauce

1 tsp. fresh grated ginger

2 cloves garlic, minced

¼ cup brown sugar

1. Mix all the ingredients together and place them in a covered glass bowl or resealable bag. Refrigerate for several hours to overnight.
2. Heat the grill to high, and grill the chicken breast for several minutes per side until it is cooked through.
3. Serve immediately with rice, grilled vegetables, and teriyaki sauce.

HIBACHI SALMON

Salmon is my favorite protein, and this way of grilling it on the hibachi is great, especially with the maple syrup.

2 lbs. salmon fillets

½ cup teriyaki sauce

1 tsp. fresh grated ginger

2 cloves garlic

¼ cup brown sugar

2 tsp. black pepper

1 Tbsp. maple syrup

1. Mix all the ingredients together in a covered glass bowl or resealable bag, and refrigerate for several hours to overnight.
2. Heat the grill to high, and grill the salmon fillets for 3–4 minutes per side until cooked through. Salmon should be homogeneous in color with white juice between the flakes.
3. Let rest for several minutes before serving.

HIBACHI STEAK

This steak should be cooked extremely fast on a hot hibachi.
Make sure the steak is sliced thin.

2 lbs. tri-tip beef, cut into ⅛-inch slices

½ cup teriyaki sauce

1 tsp. fresh grated ginger

2 cloves garlic, minced

¼ cup brown sugar

2 Tbsp. Worcestershire sauce

3 tsp. black pepper

1. Mix all the ingredients together in a covered bowl or resealable bag, and refrigerate for several hours to overnight.
2. Heat the grill to high and grill for about 1 minute per side until cooked through.
3. Let rest for several minutes before serving.

HIBACHI SHRIMP

This is a no-fuss, delicious way to grill shrimp.

2 lbs. 30 count large shrimp, peeled and deveined

½ cup teriyaki sauce

1 tsp. fresh grated ginger

2 cloves garlic, minced

¼ cup brown sugar

1. Mix all the ingredients together, and place them in the refrigerator for several hours to overnight
2. Place the shrimp on skewers.
3. Heat the grill to high and grill for 2 minutes per side until it is cooked through. The shrimp will be opaque and white when cooked through.

ASIAN ZOODLES

The best way to cook these on a hibachi or indoor grill is to lay parchment paper down on the grill and cook on top of it. The flavors will all come through without falling through the grates.

1 lb. zucchini spirals	2 Tbsp. chopped cilantro
1 lb. yam spirals	1 tsp. chili sauce
2 Tbsp. sesame oil	8 oz. rice noodles
1 Tbsp. avocado oil	¼ lb. snap peas
1 Tbsp. rice vinegar	¼ lb. shredded carrots
2 cloves garlic, minced	2 radishes, sliced thin
zest and juice of 1 lime	¼ cup Bragg's Liquid Aminos (or soy sauce)

1. Mix all of the ingredients together, and chill them in the fridge for 20 minutes to 3 hours.
2. Heat up the grill to high and cover with parchment paper.
3. Spray the paper with spray oil.
4. Pour the contents of the mix onto the grill.
5. Grill and stir frequently until the noodles and veggies are tender.

MEDITERRANEAN

IF I COULD ONLY EAT ONE type of food the rest of my life, this would be it. I Love Mediterranean food. It is such a good balance of deep seasonings and fresh ingredients.

CHICKEN SHAWARMA 86

CHICKEN SOUVLAKI 88

LAMB SOUVLAKI 89

VEGETARIAN GYROS 90

MOROCCAN LAMB KABOBS 91

CHICKEN SHAWARMA

This quintessential Middle Eastern dish is so good eaten with hummus and fresh greens.

boneless skinless chicken thighs, cut into chunks

1 Tbsp. cumin

1 Tbsp. coriander

1 Tbsp. cardamom

2 tsp. smoked paprika

1 tsp. black pepper

2 tsp. salt

2 cloves garlic, minced

zest and juice of 1 lemon

¼ cup olive oil

1. Mix all of the ingredients together, and place them in the refrigerator for several hours to overnight.
2. Put all the chicken pieces onto skewers, leaving space between the pieces.
3. Heat the grill to high, and grill the skewers for 4–5 minutes per side until cooked through.
4. Let the meat relax for 5 minutes before serving.

CHICKEN SOUVLAKI

I love good souvlaki in a pita shell served with a tzatziki sauce and lemon rice.

2 lbs. chicken breasts, cut into strips

5 garlic cloves, minced

zest and juice of 2 lemons

3 sprigs fresh oregano

¼ cup olive oil

sea salt to taste

1. Mix all of the ingredients together and place them in the refrigerator for several hours to overnight.
2. Put all the chicken pieces onto skewers, leaving space between the pieces.
3. Heat the grill to high and grill the skewers for several minutes per side until it is cooked through.
4. Let the chicken relax for 5 minutes before serving.

LAMB SOUVLAKI

This classic Greek dish is best served with lemon rice and tabouli.

2 lbs. lamb, cut into ⅛-inch strips

5 garlic cloves, minced

zest and juice of 2 lemons

3 sprigs fresh oregano

¼ cup olive oil

sea salt to taste

1. Mix all of the ingredients together, and place them in the refrigerator for several hours to overnight.
2. Put all the lamb pieces onto skewers, leaving space between the pieces.
3. Heat the grill to high, and grill the skewers for 3–4 minutes per side until it is cooked through.
4. Let the meat relax for 5 minutes before serving.

VEGETARIAN GYROS

This is a fun and delicious take on gyros without the meat.

1 cup canned chickpeas, rinsed and drained

3 cups zucchini ribbons

1 small onion, slivered

zest and juice of 2 lemons

4 cloves garlic, minced

½ tsp. cumin

1 tsp. smoked sweet paprika

1 tsp. sea salt

pita bread

olive oil

2 sprigs mint, chopped (garnish)

parsley, chopped (garnish)

plain yogurt (garnish)

fresh tomatoes, diced (garnish)

1. Mix the chickpeas, zucchini, and onions together with the lemons, garlic, and seasonings. Let relax for 20–30 minutes.
2. Heat the grill to high and place some parchment paper down on it. Spray the parchment paper with spray oil.
3. Grill the veggies for 15 minutes or until the onions are clear and the zucchini is tender.
4. Lightly coat the outside of the pitas with olive oil. Fill the pitas with the mixture and return the pitas to the grill for a couple of minutes until they are warm through and are just starting to crisp around the edges.
5. Garnish as desired with the mint, parsley, yogurt, and tomatoes.

MOROCCAN LAMB KABOBS

I have always dreamed of being in Morocco and walking the outdoor markets of Marrakech, smelling the lamb grilled on wood coals. This recipe was created from that inspiration.

2 lbs. lamb, cut into ⅛-inch strips

6 garlic cloves, minced

½ cup olive oil

1 Tbsp. coriander

2 tsp. cumin

zest and juice of 2 lemons

2 Tbsp. fresh mint, chopped

3 tsp. salt

2 tsp. black pepper

apricot jam

1. Mix all of the ingredients except for the apricot jam together, and place in the refrigerator for several hours to overnight.
2. Put all the lambs pieces onto skewers, leaving space between the pieces.
3. Heat the grill to high, and grill the skewers for 3–4 minutes per side until cooked through.
4. Brush the apricot jam on the lamb, and grill for less than 1 minute on each side to set the glaze.
5. Let the meat relax for 5 minutes before serving.

MORE WORLD GRILLING FLAVORS

THESE INDOOR GRILLED RECIPES have been inspired by traditional dishes from around the world. These are fun recipes that can enhance the variety of dishes in your home.

TANDOOR-INSPIRED CHICKEN (INDIA)

Tandoor ovens are wood-fired clay ovens that are known for locking a beautiful smoky flavor into food. Though the indoor grill can't replicate the tandoor grill, the seasonings can create an exciting dish.

3 lbs. chicken legs, skin removed

3 Tbsp. vegetable oil

1 tsp. ground coriander

1 tsp. ground cumin

1 tsp. ground turmeric

1 Tbsp. garam masala

1 Tbsp. smoked sweet paprika

1 cup plain yogurt

juice of 1 lemon

4 garlic cloves, minced

2 Tbsp. minced fresh ginger

1 tsp. salt

1. Mix all of the ingredients together, and place them in the refrigerator for several hours to overnight.
2. Put all the chicken pieces onto skewers, leaving space between the pieces.
3. Heat the grill to high, and grill the skewers for 4–5 minutes per side until the chicken is cooked through.
4. Let the chicken relax for 5 minutes before serving.

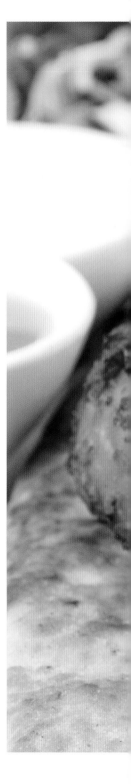

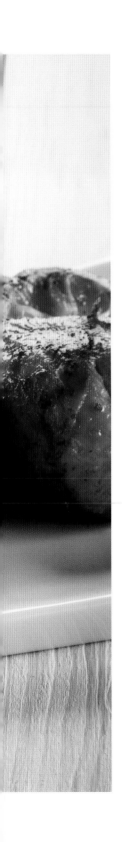

JERKED CHICKEN (JAMAICA)

I tried jerk spices for the first time when I was nineteen. I am still amazed at the depth of flavor achieved from the Caribbean. This recipe is inspired by that cuisine.

3 lbs. chicken legs

½ tsp. nutmeg

1 tsp. cinnamon

1 Tbsp. coriander

1 tsp. whole cloves

½ tsp. allspice

1 tsp. black peppercorns

1 bunch scallions, chopped

1 large onion, roughly chopped

2 habanero peppers, veined, seeded, and chopped

10 sprigs thyme, stripped

8 garlic cloves, minced

zest and juice of 8 limes

1 cup soy sauce

½ cup brown sugar

1. Mix all of the ingredients together except the chicken, run them through a food processor, and place them in the refrigerator with the chicken for several hours to overnight.
2. Put all the chicken pieces onto skewers, leaving space between the pieces.
3. Heat the grill to high, and grill the skewers for 4–5 minutes per side until the chicken is cooked through.
4. Let the meat relax for 5 minutes before serving.

CRUSTED SEARED AHI (POLYNESIA)

Ahi tuna is so amazing, especially when cooked with this sweet marinade and crust. This recipe is inspired by the fresh fish and flavors of the Polynesian islands.

2 lbs. ahi tuna fillets, cut 1.5 inches thick

½ cup soy sauce

¼ cup mirin

½ cup brown sugar

½ cup chopped fresh pineapple

sesame seeds

panko

1. Cook the soy sauce, mirin, sugar, and pineapple in a saucepan on medium until it is slightly thickened.
2. Let the sauce cool, and place the fish in the sauce. Set in the fridge for several hours.
3. Heat up the grill to high and spray with oil.
4. Cook the fillets for 2 minutes per side, then sprinkle both sides with sesame seeds and panko and grill for 1 minute more per side.
5. Let the tuna relax, and slice it thin to serve. It should be rare in the middle.

BRATS AND KRAUT (GERMANY)

I believe brats already have a huge grill following, but it seemed natural to include it in this book. This recipe is simple but inspired from German brats.

2 lbs. fresh ground brats

1 large sweet onion, cut into slivers

1 red bell pepper, seeded, veined, and slivered

brown mustard (for garnish)

sauerkraut (for garnish)

1. Heat the grill to high. Cover the grill with parchment paper, spray with spray oil, and add the brats, onion, and bell pepper.
2. Grill together until the brat is swollen and cooked through.
3. Remove from heat, and serve garnished with brown mustard and sauerkraut.

KOTLETY (RUSSIA)

Most people don't consider Russia a place for grilling—I certainly would not have. Grilling is so primal and universal that it is found in every corner of the world. This recipe is inspired by a grilled ground meat popular in Russia. Serve this with root vegetables like carrots, beets, or potatoes.

1 lb. ground beef

1 lb. ground pork

1 cup whole wheat bread crumbs

⅓ cup milk

1 tsp. sea salt

1 tsp. ground black pepper

2 tsp. smoked sweet paprika

2 cloves garlic, minced

1 small sweet onion, grated

2 eggs

1. Mix all of the ingredients together. Form mixture into small patties about ½ inch thick.
2. Heat the grill to high.
3. Cook the patties for several minutes per side until cooked through. The internal temperature should reach 155 degrees.
4. Let the meat rest for several minutes before serving with root vegetables.

SUYA (WEST AFRICA)

Popular in Nigeria and nearby regions, this flavorful beef is grilled to perfection. What makes it unique is the use of roasted peanuts in the spice blend. This recipe is inspired by that region.

3 lbs. steak strips, sliced ¼ inch thick lengthwise

1 onion, roughly chopped

4 cloves garlic, peeled

3 tsp. smoked sweet paprika

½ cup roasted peanuts

¼ cup olive oil

2 tsp. sea salt

1 tsp. black pepper

1 tsp. cayenne pepper

½ tsp. cumin

1. Mix all the ingredients except the beef together, and pulse them in a blender until they create a rough mix.
2. Cover the steak strips with the mix, and let the beef relax in the seasoning in the refrigerator for several hours.
3. Skewer the meat onto water-soaked wooden skewers.
4. Heat the grill to high, and grill the meat for 2 minutes per side. Finish it to your desired amount of doneness.
5. Let the meat relax for several minutes before serving.

KOFTA (ARMENIA)

My family had Armenian friends growing up, and I loved the get-togethers and trying the food. This recipe is inspired from the beautiful grilled kebab dishes I tried. Serve this on pita bread.

1 lb. ground beef

1 lb. ground lamb

1 medium yellow onion, chopped

2 garlic cloves, minced

1 bunch parsley, stems removed, chopped

1 slice of bread, toasted until browned and then crumbled

2 tsp. sea salt

1½ tsp. ground allspice

½ tsp. cayenne pepper

1 tsp. cardamom

½ tsp. ground nutmeg

1 tsp. smoked sweet paprika

1. Mix all the ingredients together, and form the meat around skewers.
2. Heat the grill to high and grill the skewers for 4–5 minutes per side until it is cooked through.
3. Let the meat relax for a few minutes before serving on pita bread.

NORWEGIAN SALMON (NORWAY)

This is a great way to grill salmon. This recipe is inspired from some Norwegian salmon dishes I have tried. The sweetness caramelizes on the grill and perfectly accents the salmon.

2 lbs. salmon fillets

1 tart apple, cut into ¼-inch cubes

½ cup golden raisins

1 Tbsp. Dijon mustard

zest and juice of 1 lemon

¼ cup olive oil

3 Tbsp. chopped flat-leaf parsley

1 tsp. sea salt

1 tsp. black pepper

1. Add all of the ingredients except the salmon to a blender and puree until it is a smooth sauce.
2. Heat the grill to high, and add the salmon, brushing the salmon with the sauce frequently. Grill until the for 3–5 minutes on each side until it is just done through.
3. Let the salmon relax for a couple of minutes before serving. Add any extra sauce desired.

SHRIMP ON THE BARBIE (AUSTRALIA)

Although I feel that cinema has a lot to do with this particular dish, it seems appropriate to include an Australian-inspired grilled dish.

3 lbs. large raw shrimp, peeled and deveined

½ lb. butter, melted

3 cloves garlic, minced

zest and juice of 1 lemon

2 tsp. sea salt

2 tsp. black pepper

¼ cup grated parmesan cheese

1. Place the shrimp on skewers.
2. Mix the remaining ingredients together and set in a bowl.
3. Heat the grill to high and grill the shrimp, brushing with the butter mixture, for 2 minutes per side until they are cooked through. They will be solid in color with white and pink tones rather than blue and gray.
4. Serve with grilled summer vegetables, grilled yellow potatoes, or grilled corn (elote).

GOURMET SANDWICHES

EVERYONE HAS HAD A GRILLED cheese sandwich, but most have never understood a true grilled cheese. With the recent popularity of paninis, the grilled sandwiches are making an appearance in our food culture. This section has some fun and fantastic grilled sandwich recipes.

MONTE CRISTO 112

LEMON SOY CHICKEN BREAST 114

BREAD CHEESE GRILLED CHEESE 115

VEGETARIAN SOURDOUGH 116

GRILLED CORNBREAD 117

GRILLED PIZZA 118

MONTE CRISTO

I have had so many variations of the monte cristo, from the deep-fried version of New Orleans to the French-toast version of Tennessee. I drew inspiration from all of them to create this grilled version.

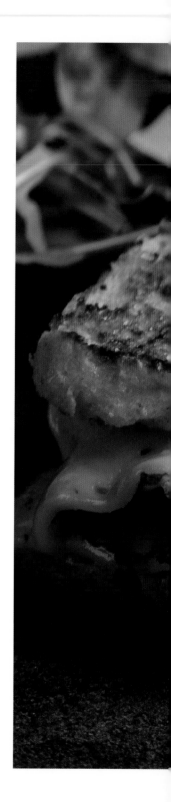

For the main sandwich

sliced ham

sliced turkey breast

swiss cheese, sliced

gruyere cheese, sliced

mixed berry jam

artisan country French bread, sliced

powdered sugar (optional)

For the custard

2 eggs

½ pint cream

1 tsp. cinnamon

¼ tsp. nutmeg

pinch of salt

1. Mix the ingredients together for the custard in a bowl and set to the side.
2. Create the sandwiches by layering the meats and cheeses and spreading the jam lightly on the bread.
3. Heat the grill up to medium.
4. Dip the sandwiches lightly into the custard and place on the grill. Grill them until the crust is golden brown on both sides and the cheese is melted.
5. Garnish lightly with powdered sugar if desired.

LEMON SOY CHICKEN BREAST

This sandwich has a great summer feel. It goes very well with corn on the cob or other grilled summer vegetables.

2 lbs. boneless chicken breasts, cut into ½-inch
    strips

½ cups soy sauce

zest and juice of 1 lemon

½ cup water

¼ cup brown sugar

1 tsp. black pepper

sourdough bread, sliced

olive oil

1. Mix the chicken, soy sauce, lemon zest and juice, brown sugar, and black pepper together, and let the mixture sit in the fridge for several hours.

2. Heat the grill to high, and grill the meat for several minutes per side until done through. The Internal temperature should reach 165 degrees.

3. Brush the outside edge of the bread lightly with olive oil, and fill the sandwich with the chicken slices. Lightly grill the sandwich until golden brown and starting to crisp.

4. Serve with mayo, cheese, lettuce, fresh sliced tomatoes, avocado slices, etc., to your taste.

BREAD CHEESE GRILLED CHEESE

This is a fun take on a gluten-free sandwich. The bread cheese is a little hard to find but totally worth it. Bread cheese is a unique ingredient found in higher-end cheese markets and islands.

For the main sandwich

3 Tbsp. olive oil

1 small red onion, sliced

½ lb. brown mushrooms, sliced

1 red pepper, veined and sliced

¼ lb. fresh baby spinach, washed

sea salt to taste

bread cheese, sliced ½ inch thick

1 Tbsp. balsamic vinegar

For the pesto

1 cup fresh basil

2 Tbsp. olive oil

½ cup pine nuts

2 cloves garlic, peeled

1 tsp. sea salt

1. Mix the ingredients together for the pesto in a food processor and pulse until it is a medium-rough consistency. Set aside.
2. In a frying pan, pour 3 tablespoons of olive oil, just to fill the bottom. Sauté the onion, mushrooms, and red pepper until the onions are clear. Add the spinach and sauté until it is uniformly dark. Add sea salt to taste.
3. Scoop the veggie mix onto the bread cheese, drizzle with balsamic, and add some pesto. Top with another slice of bread cheese.
4. Heat the grill to medium, and grill for several minutes per side until the bread cheese has grill marks.

VEGETARIAN SOURDOUGH

Admittedly, I haven't always been a fan of vegetarian cuisine, but I think it was because I tried too many that were trying to imitate meat. When I have tried vegetarian recipes that embrace the veggies, I think they are brilliantly delicious.

For the main sandwich

sweet potato planks, sliced ¼ inch thick

sweet onion, sliced thin

tomatillo, sliced thin

olive oil

sea salt to taste

sourdough bread, sliced

For the chimichurri sauce

½ cup olive oil

2 Tbsp. red wine vinegar

½ cup finely chopped parsley

3-4 cloves garlic, finely chopped or minced

2 small red chilies, deseeded and finely chopped (about 1 Tbsp. finely chopped chili)

¾ tsp. dried oregano

1 level tsp. coarse salt

pepper to taste (about ½ tsp.)

1. Add the ingredients for the chimichurri to a food processor and mix well. Set aside.
2. Grill sweet potato slices, onions and tomatillo slices on grill
3. Mix the sweet potato, onion, and tomatillo in a frying pan at high heat.
4. Pour just enough olive oil to coat the pan, and sauté until the onions are clear.
5. Add the chimichurri sauce lightly to the onion and potato mixture. Add sea salt to taste. Place the mixture between the sourdough slices. Lightly brush the outside of the sourdough with olive oil.
6. Heat the grill to medium, and grill the sandwich for several minutes on both sides until it is golden and crispy.

GRILLED CORNBREAD

This is a fun way to have cornbread. The grill adds another dimension of flavor to the cornbread. When you add a filling, you can create a grilled sandwich everyone can remember.

For the cornbread

3 eggs

1 cup buttermilk

1 cup warm water

2 cups flour

2 cups yellow cornmeal

1 cup sugar

1½ tsp. baking soda

1½ tsp. baking powder

For the filling

ham slices

gruyere cheese, sliced

fresh pico de gallo

1. Mix all of the wet ingredients for the cornbread in one bowl and the dry ingredients for the cornbread in another bowl. Fold the dry mix into the wet and combine. Be careful not to not overmix.
2. Pour the cornbread mix into a well-greased baking dish.
3. Bake at 350 degrees for about an hour or until a knife inserted comes out clean.
4. When the cornbread is cool, cut into squares, slice in half, and fill with the ham, cheese, and pico.
5. Heat the grill to medium, and grill the sandwich for a couple of minutes per side until it is golden brown and the cheese is melting.

GRILLED PIZZA

This is a very fun and delicious way to make pizza. The grill can be much hotter than the oven and create some amazing pizza. Be sure to cover the top to keep the heat in so the cheese melts.

½ cup warm water

1 Tbsp. yeast

1 tsp. salt

1 Tbsp. olive oil

1 cup flour

any traditional pizza topping ingredients desired

1. Place the warm water and yeast in a bowl. Wait for several minutes until you see the yeast begin to bloom.
2. Slowly stir in half of the flour, and mix well until smooth.
3. Stir in the salt and olive oil.
4. Slowly add in the remaining flour, and mix the dough until it is too hard to stir.
5. Knead the dough for several minutes until it is smooth and stretchy. Add flour as needed.
6. Let the dough rise for 1 hour or until it has doubled in size.
7. Punch the dough down and roll it out into the size of the pizzas you want.
8. Place the dough on parchment paper and decorate the pizza with your choice of ingredients.
9. Heat the grill to high. Place the parchment with the pizza on the grill, and cover it with tin foil.
10. Grill the pizza for several minutes until the crust is browned well and the cheese is melted.

GRILLED DESSERTS

GRILLED DESSERTS ARE becoming more popular, and with good reason—they are delicious.

GRILLED PEACHES WITH HONEY 122

STUFFED FRENCH TOAST 125

GRILLED POUND CAKE WITH BERRY COMPOTE 126

CARAMEL GRILLED PLANTAINS 129

CITRUS DARK CHOCOLATE CAKE 130

GRILLED PEACHES WITH HONEY

Peaches are my favorite fruit. I look forward to them every summer. Grilling them with honey and cinnamon and then topping them with vanilla ice cream is a real treat.

fresh peaches

fresh honey

cinnamon to taste

coconut oil

plain yogurt or ice cream for topping

1. Slice the peaches lengthwise top to bottom and remove the pits.
2. Drizzle honey on the cut side of the peach and sprinkle with cinnamon.
3. Heat the grill to medium and set the peaches sliced-side up.
4. grill peaches for a couple minutes cut side down then flip and brush with coconut oil honey and cinnamon
5. Grill for several minutes until the skin is starting to brown and pull back.
6. Serve with vanilla ice cream while still warm.

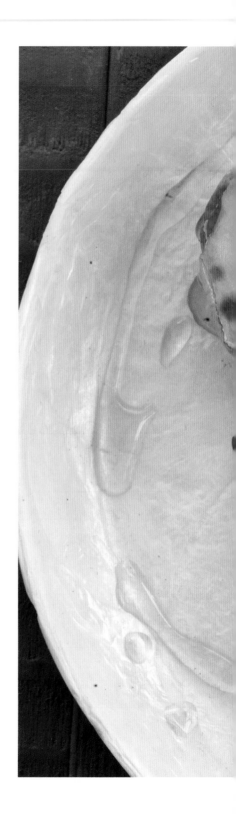

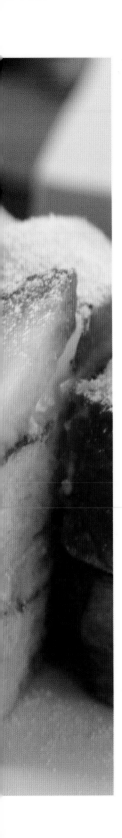

STUFFED FRENCH TOAST

This is a new twist on French toast for the indoor grill that you will enjoy! The balance of flavors is great and is sure to be a crowd pleaser.

2 loaves of French bread, cut into 1-inch slices

For the custard

¼ cup milk

1 egg

juice of ½ blood orange

3 strawberries, stemmed and hulled

pinch of ground cloves

¼ tsp. vanilla

pinch of sea salt

For the filling

¼ cup mascarpone

zest of 1 blood orange

1 tsp. real maple syrup

sliced strawberries

powdered sugar

1. Mix the custard ingredients together in a blender, and set aside in a bowl.
2. Mix the mascarpone, blood orange zest, and maple syrup together in a bowl.
3. Heat up the indoor grill to medium, and coat it with spray oil.
4. Add the mascarpone mixture and the sliced strawberries between two slices of French bread. Dip the outsides of the sandwich in the custard and drip the remaining custard off.
5. Cook for 5–6 minutes until the custard is lightly golden bronw and the bread is golden. Dust with powdered sugar and enjoy.

GRILLED POUND CAKE WITH BERRY COMPOTE

This is a unique take on pound cake that is very tasty. Make the pound cakes ahead of time, and let them set completely before grilling them.

For the pound cake

1 cup butter, softened

1 cup sugar

4 eggs

1 tsp. vanilla

pinch of salt

2 cups flour

For the compote

1 cup fresh mixed berries (any variety)

½ cup sugar

1 Tbsp. cornstarch

1. Mix the compote ingredients together in a saucepan. Bring to a boil, stirring well. Remove from the heat, and set aside.
2. In a mixing bowl, mix the butter and sugar until fluffy.
3. Add the eggs one at a time, mixing well between each egg.
4. Add the vanilla and salt.
5. Stir in the flour until well combined, but do not overmix.
6. Scoop and level the pound cake batter out onto a sheet pan.
7. Bake until the cake is golden brown.
8. Once the pound cake is cooled, cut into 3-inch squares.
9. Heat the grill to medium, and grill the pound cakes lightly. Serve warm with the compote drizzled over the top.

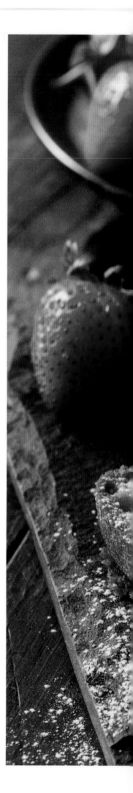

CARAMEL GRILLED PLANTAINS

I didn't know that there was a difference between a banana and a plantain as a kid. The first time I tried a plantain, I was amazed by the delicate and starchy mildness. The grill brings out the sweetness, and the glaze adds a new level to make this a great dessert.

plantains

coconut oil

raw honey

coconut cream

cinnamon

pistachios, removed from the shell and chopped

1. Peel the plantains, and slice them in half lengthwise.
2. Heat the grill to medium.
3. Brush the plantains all over with coconut oil.
4. Place the plantains on the grill and cook for 4–5 minutes per side until the plantains are tender.
5. Drizzle the plantains with honey, coconut cream, and cinnamon. Grill for another couple of minutes until the glaze is set and slightly sticky.
6. Remove from the grill and sprinkle with chopped pistachios to serve.

CITRUS DARK CHOCOLATE CAKE

This is a recipe I had fun with as a kid, filling citrus peels with cake batter and grilling them to bake the cake. The peels bake the cake well and infuse flavor into the dessert.

6 large oranges

For the cake

2 cups flour

2 cups sugar

½ cup extra dark cocoa

1 tsp. baking powder

1 tsp. baking soda

1 tsp. sea salt

1 tsp. vanilla

2 eggs

1 cup milk

½ cup fresh orange juice (from the oranges)

1 tsp. orange zest (from the oranges)

1. Cut the tops off the oranges—make sure it is from the top when the oranges are standing up on their own. With a spoon, remove the flesh, leaving hollow bowls of the peel. Reserve ½ cup of juice from the removed flesh and 1 teaspoon of zest from the previously removed tops to use in the cake batter.
2. Mix all of the cake ingredients together.
3. Carefully fill the hollow oranges half full with batter.
4. Heat the grill to medium, and set the oranges on the grill. Cover the oranges with tin foil. Grill for 15 minutes or until the cake batter is set. It will look firm when wiggled, and if you listen carefully, you can hear popping when it's done.
5. Let the cakes cool for several minutes. You can either peel them or scoop them out with a spoon to serve them.

CONCLUSION

WE HOPE YOU HAVE ENJOYED this book and have experienced great foods and expanded your abilities. Please continue to share what you have learned and continue to advocate healthier eating and great cooking techniques. We believe that we can bring the world together through great food. You can follow us for great tips, recipes, and inspiration on Instagram at @ChefMattPelton and @LiveDeliciouslyWithAviana. We look forward to your comments and inspiration. Thank you for all that you do to support us.

INDEX